Read it. Love it. Share it.

Zoe's Carousel

Tag, you're it! This book is from Zoe's Carousel, a book-sharing tradition created by Miss Duffy in honor of Zoe Falkenberg. It is now in your hands because someone else loved it and wanted you to read it. Please enjoy and then "tag" someone new!

Please visit zoescarousel.com to learn more about this project or check out Zoe's Carousel Facebook page, where you can post a pic of this book and tell us where you found it! **Have your own book to add to the carousel?** Print a label at zoescarousel.com and share it with someone new or a Little Free Library! Thanks for helping Zoe's love of reading continue to go 'round and 'round!

All Aboard

High-Speed Trains

by Jenna Lee Gleisner

Bullfrog Books

Ideas for Parents and Teachers

Bullfrog Books let children practice reading informational text at the earliest reading levels. Repetition, familiar words, and photo labels support early readers.

Before Reading

- Discuss the cover photo. What does it tell them?

- Look at the picture glossary together. Read and discuss the words.

Read the Book

- "Walk" through the book and look at the photos. Let the child ask questions. Point out the photo labels.

- Read the book to the child, or have him or her read independently.

After Reading

- Prompt the child to think more. Ask: Many high-speed trains run around the world. Would you like to ride in one?

Bullfrog Books are published by Jump!
5357 Penn Avenue South
Minneapolis, MN 55419
www.jumplibrary.com

Library of Congress Cataloging-in-Publication Data

Names: Gleisner, Jenna Lee, author.
Title: High-speed trains / Jenna Lee Gleisner.
Description: Minneapolis: Jump!, Inc., 2020.
Series: All aboard | Includes index.
Audience: Ages 5–8. | Audience: Grades K–1.
Identifiers: LCCN 2019022746 (print)
LCCN 2019022747 (ebook)
ISBN 9781645272427 (hardcover)
ISBN 9781645272434 (ebook)
Subjects: LCSH: High speed trains—Juvenile literature.
Classification: LCC TF148 .G56 2020 (print)
LCC TF148 (ebook) | DDC 385—dc23
LC record available at https://lccn.loc.gov/2019022746
LC ebook record available at https://lccn.loc.gov/2019022747

Editors: Jenna Trnka and Sally Hartfiel
Designer: Molly Ballanger

Photo Credits: Sailorr/Shutterstock, cover; TungCheung/Shutterstock, 1; pedrosala/Shutterstock, 3; aapsky/Shutterstock, 4; Blanscape/Shutterstock, 5; Xinhua/Alamy, 6–7, 15, 23bl; Juan Camilo Bernal/Shutterstock, 8–9; cyo bo/Shutterstock, 10–11; robertharding/SuperStock, 12–13, 23tl; VCG/Getty, 14, 23br; kmn-network/iStock, 16–17; Enzojz/Shutterstock, 18; best pixels/Shutterstock, 19; real444/iStock, 20–21; revers/Shutterstock, 23tr; Diego Hernan/Shutterstock, 24.

Printed in the United States of America at Corporate Graphics in North Mankato, Minnesota.

Table of Contents

Fast Trains

Zoom!

This is a high-speed train.

These trains go fast!
Cool!

They carry passengers.

This train is in China.
It is the fastest one
in the world.

It goes 267 miles
(430 kilometers)
per hour.

Wow!

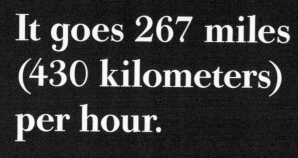

It is a maglev train.

It does not have wheels.

It uses magnets.

It floats!

This train is in China, too.
It has wheels.
It runs on tracks.

track

It is still very fast!

Where can you ride one?
This one is in Germany.

This one is in France.

It goes to Italy.

It takes just seven hours!

Nice!

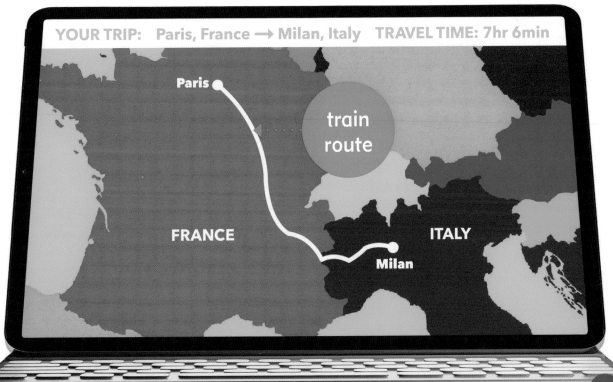

YOUR TRIP: Paris, France → Milan, Italy   TRAVEL TIME: 7hr 6min

Paris

train route

FRANCE

ITALY

Milan

These trains take us places fast!

Do you want to ride one?

How a Maglev Train Floats

A magnet has a north and south pole. Opposite poles stick together. Like poles push away from one another. This is how maglev trains float.

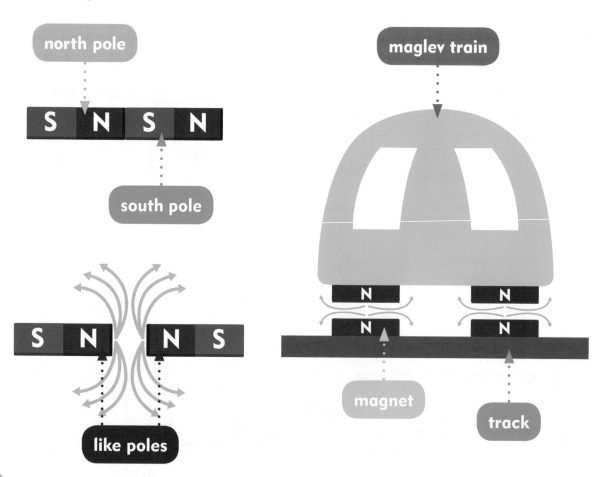

Picture Glossary

maglev train
Short for magnetic levitation train. A floating vehicle that is supported by magnets.

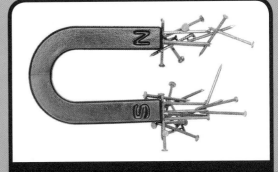

magnets
Pieces of metal that attract iron or steel. Magnets have two ends, or poles, called north and south.

passengers
People besides the driver who travel in a vehicle.

tracks
Rails or sets of rails for vehicles, such as trains, to run on.

Index

To Learn More

Finding more information is as easy as 1, 2, 3.

❶ Go to www.factsurfer.com

❷ Enter "high-speedtrains" into the search box.

❸ Choose your book to see a list of websites.